the A.B.Cs of Christmas

Message from the Author:

Wow, this has been the biggest Creative Faith project I have ever tackled. Many nights, hours and time spent praying, and pouring over the Bible for this book. I am so excited it is in your hands.

I want to give a special thank you to my parents who helped me edit this book. I appreciate all your love and support when it comes to this project and all the God-sized dreams He has placed on my heart.

Remember the importance of reading the context around the verses I mention in this devotion book as you are reading God's Word.

I pray as you prepare your heart for the Christmas season that you would pause and take time to listen to what God is trying to teach you. I pray He would fill your heart with joy and remind you of the true reason we celebrate: God loves us so much that He sent Jesus to earth to die for us. What magnificent love. Soak it up today and every day.

In Christ,
Hillary Krippaehne

© *October 2018* by Creative Faith & Co. Hillary Krippaehne
for personal use only // not to be copied, distributed,
altered or sold // www.creativefaithco.com

My Goals for the Christmas Season

Use this page to brainstorm some goals as you prepare for the holidays, physically, mentally, emotionally, and spiritually. Write them all down here:

A for Angel: God's Surprises

As we start on a journey to prepare our hearts for Christmas, I feel it's only fitting to begin where the Christmas story begins, too. It all started with an angel.

Read Luke 1:26-38.

In the Message version of the Bible, the angel Gabriel tells Mary God has a surprise for her: Jesus! God wants us to know He also has surprises for us. Angels are messengers for the Lord. They share news God's people need to know. Mary needed to hear God had a shockingly different direction for her life than she had ever dreamed possible.

God wants us to be reminded through the Christmas story that He has many surprises for us, too. Mary thought her life was going to go in one direction, and God had something totally different and better in store for her.

After college I moved to the Dominican Republic to teach. When my time teaching my students had finished, I began looking for other jobs. I thought maybe I would move to another country to become a missionary or a teacher. I pondered staying in the Dominican Republic to find another teaching job, but God had a completely different surprise for me. It started with a part-time summer internship at my church in Oregon. Then ,at the end of the summer, they offered me a full-time job in youth ministry. Never in my entire life did I think I would work at a church. My story is similar to Mary's: God had something different in store for me than I thought.

A for Angel: God's Surprises

1. Draw a picture of Mary, or cut out a lady from a magazine that might look like Mary. Glue the image down in this devotion book or your Bible. Draw some thought bubbles above her head illustrating what she might have been thinking when the angel was talking to her.

2. Reflect about some surprises that God has put in your life before. A job? A baby? An unexpected gift? What has He taught you through those surprises?

3. Write a prayer, asking God to help you accept the surprises He has in store for you this December.

B is for Beacon: Shine for the Lord

During my first December living on my own, I had my own Christmas tree. Before I even picked out the evergreen from the tree farm, I went to the store and purchased the prettiest and most sparkly lights I could find to wrap around the branches. I knew more than anything I wanted the tree to be wrapped in lights. My parents helped me cut down the tree and take it to my apartment. It sat right by the gigantic window to the porch, so everyone who drove by could see the glow from the tree sparkling in the night, shining for all to see.

Most evenings and mornings in the month of December I would sit in the living room and read or watch Hallmark Christmas movies next to the tree. The lights reminded me of our responsibility to shine brightly for the Lord – in December and every other day of the year.

The word "beacon" means a fire or light set up high in a prominent position as a signal or celebration. My Christmas tree was exactly that – a light set up to shine for the world, telling everyone I celebrate the fact that Jesus came to save us. Our lives need to be beacons to the dark world around us, reminding others of the joy and light that comes from God.

B is for Beacon: Shine for the Lord

1. Draw your home covered in Christmas lights or your Christmas tree shining out from the front window. Think about how your home can be a beacon to the world.
2. Read Matthew 5:14-16. Do a study and write out those verses from several different versions of the Bible. You could try the English Standard Version, the King James version, or the Message. Comparing the different versions of the Bible can help us have a deeper understanding of the text. Reflect about what God wants to teach you.

C is for Sugar Cookies: Sweet to Trust in Jesus

Every year around Christmas my mom makes her famous sugar cookies. They are requested at all the parties we attend, because everyone loves them so much. I love to eat the raw cookie dough, and my sister helps my mom frost and decorate the cookies. They taste delicious, and they are a reminder of how sweet it is to trust in the Lord during the various seasons of our lives: the good and challenging.

One of my favorite hymns is, "Tis So Sweet to Trust in Jesus." This hymn was written by Louisa M. R. Stead. This hymn was written after a tragedy struck Louisa's life. Louisa and her family went to the beach for a vacation. Her husband saw a young boy drowning in the water. He went in to save the boy, but was pulled under instead and drowned. Louisa meditated and thought about why God put this tragedy in her life as she wrote the words to this hymn. God puts hard moments in our life to remind us of how sweet, delightful, and satisfying it is to trust in Him. Always.

Read Matthew 2:13-15.

Can you imagine being in Mary and Joseph's shoes? They have the Son of God's life in their hands and King Herod wanted to kill him. They had to put immense trust in God when He told them to flee to Egypt. And trust that He would tell them when it was okay to return, but God was in control. It was safe to trust Him.

C is for Sugar Cookies: Sweet to Trust in Jesus

1. Listen to the hymn "Tis So Sweet to Trust in Jesus." Write out the lyrics that impact you the most.

2. Draw a picture of your favorite Christmas sweet treat. Sugar cookies? Apple pie? As you draw, think about how sweet, delightful, and satisfying it is to trust in God.

3. Write about a challenging time you have experienced and reflect on it as you eat a sugar cookie. How has it been sweet to trust in the Lord during that difficult time?

D is for Dare: Be Bold and Share

It fascinates me to look at all the different people in the story of Jesus' birth. The shepherds are an interesting group of characters to be the first people the Bible mentions visit baby Jesus. I do not think the shepherds were well dressed, and they probably did not smell good after living in the fields for so long with their sheep. They were not the richest people in the land. They were probably not educated, but they urgently went to visit Jesus. They left right away to find him. It's what they do afterward that really gets me thinking.

In Luke 2:17-18 we learn after visiting Jesus the shepherds went out and told everyone about him. They shared with people what the angels said and how they met the son of God. What an example for all of us. We need to dare to share the good news about the birth of Jesus with others. We need to have the boldness and courage to share about who Jesus is and what he has done to transform our lives, just like the shepherds.

We can be confident because if God can use the shepherds to share about Jesus, He can use us, too. We don't need to be well educated, or even to have read the whole Bible. We don't have to be rich or smell good to tell other people about Jesus. This Christmas I dare you to be bold and talk with others about the reason we celebrate: Jesus!

D is for Dare: Be Bold and Share

1. Read Isaiah 52:7 and Romans 10:15. Take some time to journal both pages in your Bible or in a notebook. Think about the shepherd's feet and your feet. How are both sharing the Good News about Jesus?
2. Create an acronym using the word DARE to remind you the importance of being bold and spreading the good news.
3. Read Psalm 105:1 and write a prayer, asking God to help you have confidence and courage to dare to share about Him to all the nations.

E is for Extravagant Gifts: Where's My Money?

One Christmas I decided I really wanted to bless my parents and my sister, so I spent more money than I should have based on what sat in my bank account. I wanted to impress them and let them know I loved them through purchasing everything I could for them. The monetary amount I spent was more important than getting and giving gifts from the heart. I wanted to make sure I spent "enough" on each of them, or that I had spent more on them than they had on me. Christmas became a transaction instead of a time to give extravagant gifts of love. I wasn't pausing to think about what they would like best or what would put a smile on their face. I was emptying my bank account without stopping to think about why or what I was doing.

Solomon was a man from the Bible who knew what it was like to have extravagant amounts of money. He was one of the richest kings in the Bible. He had fancy palaces and lots of money. However, as he wrote the book of Ecclesiastes, he reflected in his old age about what he learned. In Ecclesiastes 5:10, he talks about the fact that wealth does not bring happiness.

I thought these Christmas gifts would bring me happiness and bring my family happiness. The only thing in life that will bring us true contentment, joy and lasting happiness is Jesus. His extravagant love for us is the very best extravagant gift we could give or receive this Christmas.

E is for Extravagant Gifts: Where's My Money?

1. Read 1 Timothy 6:7. Use this verse and reflect about the kinds of gifts you should give others this Christmas.
2. Spend some time in prayer before you go out to do Christmas shopping this year. Think about what you could hand make for someone, or think of an experience you could do together instead of spending hundreds of dollars on gifts.
3. Use stamps, stickers, or hand lettering to write out "extravagant love." How does this phrase connect with what we learned today?

F is for Frankincense: the Meaning behind the Oil

Frankincense. Gold. Myrrh. Three meaningful gifts. The Bible tells us the wise men brought these three items to Jesus.

Read Matthew 2:11.

When my sister and I were little, my mom purchased a book that explained this part of the Christmas story, about the three gifts from the wise men. On the side of the book there was a little box with three mini bottles. The bottles held frankincense, gold and myrrh floating in liquid. My sister and I would take turns flipping the little bottles and watching the elements move around in the glass vials as we read about the wise men and their gifts.

I want to dive into the deeper meaning behind one of those presents. As I began researching, I discovered frankincense is supposed to help with anxiety and stress. It's supposed to reduce pain and help with immunity. I can imagine Mary was probably stressed about raising the son of God, and maybe she needed some help to calm her nerves. Perhaps the frankincense was give to her for that purpose. December can be an extremely stressful time of year with an endless list of things to do. Perhaps God wants to remind us that He offers us peace. We can hand Him our burdens, anxiety and stress every day.

I also discovered frankincense oil is from a tree mostly found in Somalia. It is a unique tree because it grows with little soil in really dry and barren lands. This is symbolic to Jesus' life and the lives of others in the Bible. With God's help, He can do big things with few resources. Mary, she was a virgin when she became pregnant with Jesus, and that shows us how God can do the impossible. He can make something grow out of nothing. We learn about Elizabeth and Zechariah in Luke 1. God made a baby grow inside of Elizabeth even though she was older and thought she could not have children. God is doing the same thing in our lives: He is making things grow in the middle of the desert. He is making ways for us in the wasteland where we never thought there could be growth. Do not give up. God is in the business of making things grow in the middle of the impossible.

F is for Frankincense: the Meaning behind the Oil

1. Read 2 Corinthians 2:15 and journal about how God wants our lives to be a pleasing aroma.
2. Read Isaiah 43:19. Draw a picture to help you remember this verse.
3. Find some real frankincense oil today and smell it. Maybe even rub a little on this page. Draw a picture of a bottle of oils to remind you of the meaning of Frankincense this Christmas.

G is for Gingerbread House: Home Sweet Home

My family has many traditions around Christmas time, but one of our *sweetest* is decorating a gingerbread house. We purchase one that is already together since it can be challenging to get the pieces to bind. My sister and I use licorice for the Christmas lights and chocolate bars for the windows and green gum drop candies for the trees. My sister studied to be an engineer, so her side always looks slightly more precise than mine, but we have fun decorating the sweet house.

Read Joshua 24:15.

When people enter your home during the year, but especially around Christmas time, what is it like? How do they feel when they arrive? Can people tell it's a home of the Lord? Can people see that you serve God in your house?

My sister and I spend several hours sitting around the kitchen table adding frosting and various candies to our gingerbread house. We take time to make the outside look nice. We should spend time making our real homes and living spaces into places where people feel welcomed and loved, too.

G is for Gingerbread House: Home Sweet Home

1. Write "home sweet home" on a sign on your page. Reflect about your sweet home. When people enter, can they tell it's a place of the Lord?
2. Draw a picture of a gingerbread house. Decorate it as you think about serving the Lord in your home. You could also purchase a gingerbread house kit and make one with your family and talk about how your family could use your house to serve the Lord.
3. Read and write out Psalm 127:1 or Hebrews 3:4 as you reflect about the theme of God dwelling in your house.

H is for Hospitality: Make the Time

Right after Mary found out she was pregnant, she immediately left to go stay with her relative, Elizabeth. The Bible tells us that Elizabeth let Mary stay with her for three months. Elizabeth became miraculously pregnant right before Mary. That's a long time to have a house guest, especially since Elizabeth was also pregnant.

Houseguests are a lot of work. When I was younger, some of my mom's siblings lived out of state, so they would stay with us during Christmas. I absolutely loved having my cool aunts and uncles stay at our house, but looking back, I now realize how much work it is to host people. First you need to clean the house, and then set up where they will sleep. Once they arrive, it means making special meals and entertaining them. After they leave, you have to clean up after them. My family normally would just stay a few days. I cannot imagine Mary staying with Elizabeth for three whole months.

In 1 Peter 4:9, we learn that we are to be hospitable without grumbling or complaining. Have you ever complained about having people over? Whether it's just for an evening dinner or for a weekend stay? I know I definitely have. Elizabeth is a perfect example for us of how to open your door and welcome people who need a little extra care and love this Christmas.

H is for Hospitality: Make the Time

1. Read 1 Timothy 5:10. Can people read this verse and say the same thing about you? Are you known for your good deeds like showing hospitality and washing the feet of the Lord's people? Think of some ways you could do better showing hospitality to others.
2. Draw an open door and think about how you can open your door to people this December. How can you keep this same mentality of having an open door year round to people around you?

I is for I Heard the Bells on Christmas Day: Peace in Troubled Times

I work full time at my church, and one morning in December we sat at our staff meeting talking about the poem/hymn, "I Heard the Bells on Christmas Day." We begin each staff meeting with a spiritual thought. Pastor Doug shared how Henry Wadsworth Longfellow's wife tragically died after her dress caught on fire. Then, one of his sons went off to fight in the Civil War and became seriously injured. We learned Longfellow wrote this poem as he reflected on Christmas day hearing the bells ring. Longfellow watched as people celebrated, however; he was troubled and tormented as he only saw violence and tragedy in life.

This song had never been a favorite of mine, but as I learned the history behind the lyrics, I realized how Longfellow used his words to express how he felt. He struggled to see God's goodness in the middle of a hard time. Many of us can relate to how Longfellow felt. The song became so much more personal after hearing about Longfellow's life and challenges.

If you read the lyrics to this poem, you'll see how Longfellow is essentially saying there is no peace on earth. Can we relate in our world today? However; we have something more powerful than our circumstances. We have someone more powerful on our side: Jesus! He is the reason we can celebrate no matter what is happening in our lives.

Read Romans 5:1.

God's peace passes our understanding. It comes from hope in Jesus Christ. Even when sad things happen in our lives, we can remember we have an anchor of hope and peace in the midst of the storm.

I is for I Heard the Bells on Christmas Day: Peace in Troubled Times

1. Look up the lyrics to the song and write the lines that speak to your heart the most.
2. Are you in the middle of dark times? Write out a prayer asking God to fill you with His peace this December.
3. Listen to the Casting Crowns version of "I Heard the Bells on Christmas Day." How can you see that Casting Crowns turned the song into a joyful melody instead of the dark lyrics of Longfellow?
4. Read Luke 2:14. Journal the angel's announcement using a globe or picture of the world.

J is for Jingle Bells: Making Noise for the Lord

I always love when my mom puts up all the Christmas decorations. One of my favorite decorations is a small jingle bell wreath that has been a part of our décor since I was a little girl. Mom loops this special adornment around the front door handle. The wreath makes such a pleasant and beautiful noise every time someone comes into the house or leaves.

Read through Luke chapter 1.

In this chapter, two people learn grand news about miraculous pregnancies. The first person is Mary, the mother of Jesus. The second is Elizabeth. Mary went to visit her relative Elizabeth who was also pregnant. As soon as Mary sees Elizabeth, Elizabeth's baby leaps for joy. Elizabeth shares this with Mary, and Mary bursts into song. What an example for us, too. When we hear news, good or bad, we should rejoice because it is the will of God. We can sing for joy because God is with us no matter what is happening in our lives. We can shake jingle bells and remind ourselves that joy always comes in the morning, no matter the storm we are in right now. At the end of Luke chapter 1, Elizabeth's husband Zechariah also bursts into song over his baby like Mary. He praises God for what He did and thanks God for His mercy.

The word praise means to express thankfulness to God because of His good character. The Bible reminds us in Romans 8:28 that God works all things for our good. That truth is found in God's Word. No matter your circumstances, you can sing because God is good. He is a good Father. If you are in a beautiful time of celebration like Zechariah and Mary, sing for joy. If you are struggling and in a dark time, I would encourage you to try and sing for joy today too. Even in the midst of a storm, you are not alone. You can find reasons to praise and thank God no matter what is going on in your life.

J is for Jingle Bells: Making Noise for the Lord

1. Read Psalm 100. Write out the key words and phrases that jump out to you from this chapter in the Bible.

2. What are similarities you see between Zechariah's song and Mary's? Journal about it.

3. Find some jingle bells around your house or at the store today. Shake them and really listen to the sound. Try and paint or draw what you hear. What does that joy look like when it's creatively expressed on a page?

K is for Kindness: Shower Others with Blessings

Running my Creative Faith business requires a great deal of time in the post office waiting in line. I get to watch many people interact with the employees of the United States Postal Service. Many aren't nice to the post office workers, especially around the holidays. The lines are extra-long and people's patience is thin. The post office staff is simply trying to do their best with their resources and staff.

One year I put together a Christmas gift basket full of chocolate, fruit and cheese to bless the workers at the post office where I go to mail my Creative Faith shipments. As I walked up to the counter with the basket, they were wondering how I was going to mail it since it was not in a box. They were surprised to learn the treats were for them. It was a simple way to put a smile on someone else's face.

The Bible talks about loving those around you. We shine Jesus' love when we give a surprise gift, or serve someone in an unexpected way. In 1 John 4:19, we learn that God loves us, and in return, we can show His love and kindness to others around us.

K is for Kindness: Shower Others with Blessings

1. Think about who you interact with on a daily basis who could use some extra special love. Maybe the garbage man, or your grocery cashier. Who can you bless today with kindness?
2. Google "kindness calendar ideas" and put together a list of activities you can do each day for the rest of the month of December to go out of your way to bless those around you.
3. Read Proverbs 3:3 in the New Living Translation. Get out your craft supplies and make a necklace that says the word "kindness" on it, or draw a picture of one. Think about how you could literally tie it around your neck to remind you to be kind to others.

L is for Lonely: God is with you

Have you seen the movie, *the Nativity Story*? It does a great job showing what the beginning part of the Christmas story might have been like. When Mary found out she was going to have a baby, there was much scandal and intrigue. I doubt Mary's friends stuck by her during that time. After that, Mary and Joseph went on a journey to Bethlehem where Joseph's family lived. Mary was all by herself there, too.

Read Luke 2:7.

This Bible verse says Mary wrapped Jesus in cloth and laid him in a manger. The Bible does not talk about who was with them that evening when Jesus was born, but I would imagine if Mary was the one wrapping her baby up, she probably did not have a lot of help giving birth. What a challenging situation. Mary must have felt extremely lonely.

When I feel lonely, I remember that God is always with me. When I first moved to the Dominican Republic to teach, I had no friends. Many evenings I cried in my bedroom because I was all by myself in a foreign country. But then I began spending time prayer journaling and reading my Bible. I felt less lonely because I remembered God was there with me, wrapping His loving arms around me. James 4:8 tells us that we need to draw near to the Lord. Sometimes I think back on that challenging season, and I realize God did that on purpose to pull me closer to Him because He was all I had.

Read 1 Thessalonians 5:11. Read Hebrews 10:25.
Read Ecclesiastes 4:9-12.

When I feel lonely, it can be hard to reach out to other people. But God has called us into community. He wants us to be around others and share life with people. He created us for relationships, with Him and with others. Don't forget this truth!

L is for Lonely: God is with you

1. Journal about loneliness. Do you feel lonely this holiday season? What can you do to change that?
2. Think about someone in your community who might be lonely this Christmas. How can you make them feel included this Christmas?
3. Read Isaiah 41:10. Write a prayer to God, asking Him to help you feel less lonely this Christmas. Remind yourself that He is always with you!

M is for Movies: Secret Lessons from God

My parents, sister and I have certain movies we watch every November and December. One of our favorite family movies we watch each year is Home Alone. For those of you who have never seen it before, the movie is about a family who forgets their son on Christmas vacation. The whole family ends up in France for Christmas, and the main character, an elementary school boy named Kevin, accidentally gets left behind in their home in Chicago. Kevin has all sorts of adventures, but the parents forgot their son.

There are 400 years of silence in the middle of the Old and New Testaments in the Bible. Can you imagine living in those years? No one heard from God. It seemed as though He forgot His children. But then in Luke 1, BOOM, we hear from Him again. Angels begin talking and the Son of God starts moving. In Luke 1:54 and Luke 1:72, both Mary and Zechariah mention the remembrance of God. God didn't forget the covenant He made with Abraham. God didn't forget about His children.

In the chaos of the holiday season, what are you forgetting this Christmas? Are there holiday events you have forgotten to attend? Have you forgotten to purchase someone a gift or forgotten to clean your bathroom before guests came over? Have you forgotten to thank God in the midst of the chaos? Have you forgotten God's goodness in the middle of a challenging storm? Take some time today to simple remember God.

M is for Movies: Secret Lessons from God

1. Journal about a time when you forgot something or someone. How did it feel? What did you do? What did God teach you through that moment?
2. Do you feel like God has forgotten you? Pause and pray, asking God to speak to your heart today and remind you of His presence.
3. Illustrate a picture of your favorite Christmas movie. Think about the plot line and characters. What can God teach you about Him through the story?

N is for Notes: Say "Thank You"

Thank you: what a simple phrase. I grew up writing thank you notes for every gift I was given. A few days after Christmas, my mom would sit us down at the kitchen table with a fresh stack of new thank you cards. We had a list of everyone who gave us presents, and we would spend time writing notes to our aunts, uncles, grandparents, and friends who blessed us with something over Christmas. My sister and I would hunker down and write and write.

Many people don't write thank you notes anymore. There have been many times when I have given someone a gift never to hear even a verbal thank you, let alone a special note. Thank you notes show appreciation and gratitude. They show you care enough to take a few moments to say thanks.

Read Luke 1:5-18.

While Zechariah is in the temple giving an offering, an angel tells him his wife will become pregnant. Instead of thanking and praising God, Zechariah questions the angel. He doubts and wonders how that could even happen. A severe consequence occurs because of his lack of belief and gratitude: Zechariah is struck mute for the length of Elizabeth's pregnancy.

Read Luke 1:24-25.

Elizabeth did not question the Lord when she found out she was pregnant. She recognized and praised and thanked the Lord for giving her a child. Let's take on the spirit and attitude of Elizabeth, thanking God for what He has given us and thanking others, as well.

N is for Notes: Say "Thank You"

1. How can you shower people with gratitude? Write a thank you note to someone who has blessed you with a physical gift, or simply shown you love or kindness.
2. Write a special thank you note to God, expressing gratitude for all He has given you.
3. Read Colossians 3:15-17 and reflect about how this chapter from the Bible connects with the topic of thank you notes.

O is for Our Offenses: Wreath and Crown of Love

My Grandfather owns a Christmas tree farm, and most years in high school and college I helped selling the trees. We would make small Charlie Brown Christmas trees, as well as swags and wreaths to sell. Often the Christmas wreaths had holly between the tree branches. Wreaths represent and symbolize the crown of thorns Jesus wore on his head when he died on the cross to cover our sins – our offenses.

Read Romans 3:23.

We have all sinned. Our lives are full of offenses. Every day we fail and do things we should not do. Every day we think things we should not think. Every day we disobey God. That is why God sent Jesus to the world.

Read Matthew 27:29.

The soldiers twisted together the crown of thorns, just like we twist together branches to create wreaths that we hang on doors for the month of December. This crown of thorns was meant to mock Jesus. Jesus died to save even those soldiers. We can celebrate this Christmas, remembering that even though we fail daily, God still loves us.

Read 1 Peter 2:9.

The crown and wreath represent God chose us. He loves us. We are His princesses and princes. When you see a wreath this Christmas, pause and think about Jesus' crown of thorns on the cross and what it means for your life that he died to cover your offenses.

O is for Our Offenses: Wreath and Crown of Love

1. Draw a picture of a wreath on this page to remind yourself that Jesus wore a wreath on his head to die for our offenses and wrongs.
2. Try gathering materials to make your own wreath for your door instead of just purchasing one this year. As you put it together, meditate on the gift of salvation that God loves you so much that He sent Jesus to die for you on the cross.
3. Read John 19:2-5, and Mark 15:17. Think about how the different authors told the story of Jesus and his crown of thorns.

P stands for Perfectly Imperfect: Letting Go this Christmas

My first Christmas living on my own in an apartment, I was extremely excited to decorate for the season. I purchased white twinkle lights for my tree, but I also decided to hang some on the inside of my kitchen window. I did not take the time to measure where the lights should go in order to be evenly spaced around the window. The lights were sagging a little bit between the hooks, but I liked how they looked anyway. They were perfectly imperfect.

Would you describe yourself as a perfectionist? Sometimes we can spend an excessive amount of time trying to perfect everything around us. From making sure our Christmas lights are hung perfectly, to perfectly wrapping every single Christmas gift, to perfectly dressing our children, or spending ample amounts of time dressing ourselves. Think about how that time could be spent doing other things, like enjoying time with family, or reading the Bible, or serving those around us instead of fighting the perfectionism.

Read Galatians 1:10.

When we spend much time seeking perfection, who are we trying to impress? Most of the time the answer is those around us. We want to make sure people think we live perfect lives. I imagine it makes God sad to see us waste our precious time worrying about such trivial things. Pause today and check your heart to see if you are struggling to make your Christmas too perfect. Ask God to help you with this struggle.

P stands for Perfectly Imperfect: Letting Go this Christmas

1. What parts of Christmas do you try to make "too" perfect? How can you release those worries to God this Christmas season?

2. Read Colossians 3:2. Reflect about how you might set your eyes on Christ this Christmas instead of worrying about how perfect everything should look.

3. Use stamps, stickers, or your hand lettering to write out the phrase "Let go" on the page as a reminder to release the perfectionism of the holidays.

Q is for Quest: Journeying with Jesus

Let's ponder the most epic quest found in the story of the birth of Jesus: Mary and Joseph traveling to Bethlehem. Can you imagine being pregnant and spending a week walking or on a donkey making your way to another town? What a challenge. We also have poor Joseph, trying to provide for and lead his family through a difficult journey.

Read Luke 2:1-6.

This journey for Mary and Joseph would have been around 80 miles. It would have be a long and expensive journey for the young couple. I am sure God used this trip to help Mary and Joseph get to know one another better. Whenever I have taken a road trip or vacation with someone, I got to know them better by the end of the journey. I imagine Mary and Joseph had to lean on the Lord for provisions during the trip, and God would have used the quest to bring them closer to Him, trusting Him.

Read Matthew 2:13-15.

After the magi went to visit Jesus, an angel told Joseph in a dream he had to take his family to Egypt to escape King Herod's plan to kill all the babies. The young family had another epic quest of around 40 miles where they had to lean on the Lord for support and help.

Read Matthew 2:19-23.

Once King Herod had passed away, Joseph was directed to take his family to Nazareth, another long journey of over 100 miles. Can you imagine this family having to move so frequently? To uproot and pack everything they had each time for another quest and journey. I remember moving to dorm rooms and apartments each year in college, and it was a great deal of work. But no matter what journey you are on with Jesus, he is with you through it all. During easy and challenging moments, God is using our quest with Him to teach us something and bring us closer in our relationship with Him.

Q is for Quest: Journeying with Jesus

1. Think about the other epic quests found in the story of the birth of Jesus: the shepherds and wise men. What does this theme from the Christmas story teach you?
2. What quest or journey does Jesus have you on right now? Draw a road and think about how you can keep your eyes fixed on Jesus during the trip.
3. Read Psalm 19:7-9 in the Message version of the Bible. Use a map on your page to think about your epic journey and quest with the Lord.

R is for Rejoice: Dancing around the Christmas Tree

Every December when I was young, I attended a special Saturday workshop with the high school dance team. It was called Dancing with the Debs since the team was the Debutants. I looked forward to the event each year where I would get the chance to hang out with cool high school girls and learn a Christmas dance routine. At the end of a half-day workshop, we performed a Christmas dance for all the parents who came to watch.

One year we danced to the song, "Rocking around the Christmas Tree." I remember the high school dance team members had a tiny Christmas tree and we danced around it. Once I became a freshman in high school, I got the opportunity to be on the dance team and create the dances for the little girls. Dance team was a huge part of my life and my December.

Read 2 Samuel 6:13-16.

I absolutely love the image of David dancing with all his might before the Lord. He danced around the ark, much like we danced around the Christmas tree. He rejoiced before the Lord with all he had. We also read in this story that his wife did not like the fact that David danced before God. Perhaps she was embarrassed. People might not understand why you are rejoicing or dancing, but praise the Lord anyway.

R is for Rejoice: Dancing around the Christmas Tree

1. Put on some of your favorite Christmas songs and take some time by yourself or with your family to dance around the Christmas tree. Don't worry about people making fun of you like David's wife. Dance anyway!
2. Look up the definition of the word "rejoice," and write the definition on this page.
3. Read Psalm 150:1-6. List of some reasons you have to be joyful this December.

S is for Snowflakes: Uniquely Created

I love the opening scene of the non-animated movie, *How the Grinch Stole Christmas*. It's another movie my family watches almost every year. Hundreds of snowflakes are cascading down, and every single one of them is a completely different shape. The scene zooms in on one snowflake, and you can observe the town of Whoville right there on the snowflake. I love how each snowflake is unique and different in that movie scene and in life, too.

God made us special and unique. There's no one else like you and me here on this earth. Each of us has unique gifts and unique mannerisms and physical traits. God created each and every one of us in a special way. Ephesians 2:10 tells us that we are a masterpiece of the Lord.

As we watch snow fall down around us this winter, whether in real life or in the movies, may we soak up and remember how unique we are, just like snowflake crystals. Just like God knits together each and every snowflake in the sky, the Bible also tells us in Psalm 139:13 He also knits us together in our mother's wombs.

When we are creating a snowball, we have to start small. As we roll the ball in the snow, it gradually gets larger. That is symbolic of us spiritually. We start with small faith but as we walk along with God, He teaches us more and more. Our faith grows and grows. Our spiritual snowflake gets bigger and bigger.

S is for Snowflakes: Uniquely Created

1. Read Matthew 10:30. Reflect on how God knows every single hair on your head, just like He knows and created every single snowflake differently.
2. Cut out a white paper snowflake and write your God-given unique traits on the snowflake to remind you how beautifully different He made you.
3. Read Isaiah 64:8. Draw a picture of God painting or creating a snowflake, just like He creates us out of clay.

T is for Town: Imagining Ourselves in Bethlehem

Have you heard the song, "O Little Town of Bethlehem"? It was inspired by a trip the author, Phillips Brooks, took to see the Holy Land when he was thirty years old. He went around Christmastime, and he got the opportunity to enjoy a five hour worship service at a church in Bethlehem on December 24th. This experience touched his heart. He reflected about how the people sang for hours upon hours praising the Lord.

Several years later, he was trying to write a song for the children to sing for the Christmas program at his church. He thought back to the evening in Bethlehem when people spent hours singing to the Lord and praising Him. This became the inspiration for the hymn, "O Little Town of Bethlehem," that was sung by the children December 1867.

I can imagine the town of Bethlehem that evening when Jesus was born. People were busy and back with their families arriving for the census. I imagine there was much socializing and hurrying about in the bustle of the day and evening. I wonder how much time the shepherds spent with Jesus, Mary and Joseph. Phillips Brooks spent five hours in church the night of Christmas Eve. How much time are we making to praise the Lord and spend time with Him this Christmas season? As you reflect on this hymn, think about how you can spend more time worshipping the Lord as we celebrate the birth of Jesus. How can your whole town sing and praise Him?

T is for Town: Imagining Ourselves in Bethlehem

1. Read Micah 5:2.
2. Look up the lyrics to the hymn, "O Little Town of Bethlehem." Write the lines and phrases God uses to touch your heart.
3. Imagine yourself in the town where Jesus was born, worshipping him. What do you think that experience would be like? Look up some pictures of the town of Bethlehem. Print them or try to recreate one on this page.

U is for Unsure: Questioning God

At the beginning of the story of the birth of Jesus, we find Joseph unsure about God's direction for his life.

Read Matthew 1:18-25.

When Joseph found out Mary was pregnant, Scripture tells us he planned to divorce her and stop the engagement. He was unsure of God's plan for him. He probably had many questions in his head. But God knows when we are unsure, and He sends reinforcements. God sent an angel to remind Joseph of His good plans for him and to explain more about what He wanted from Joseph. When Joseph woke up from the dream, he obeyed God.

When I was unsure of my career path after college, I prayed and asked God to be super clear with me and to direct me where He wanted me to go. I was unsure where He wanted me to be a teacher, so I asked Him to have a job land in my lap, even though I knew most jobs didn't work that way. But sure enough, a random Facebook message from an old teacher led to a connection that gave me my first teaching job after college.

God loves to clarify our uneasiness when we ask Him for help. Instead of trying to figure a way out of God's plans for your life, pause and ask God where He wants you to take your next steps.

U is for Unsure: Questioning God

1. Have you ever been unsure about God's direction for your life? Ask God to provide signs to show you the way. He will answer your prayer.
2. Draw arrows to remind you of who is really organizing and directing your life. When you are unsure, look upward.
3. Read James 1:5. Write the verse and draw what this means to you.

V is for Villain: the Bad Guy of the Bible

Every story has a bad guy, and the story of the birth of Jesus is no exception. Meet the world's most evil king: Herod. He killed his father-in-law, a few of his ten wives, and two of his sons. Jealousy filled his body as he perceived everyone wanted his spot on the throne. Some would call him a tyrant and he often conceived elaborate building projects, which caused him to excessively tax the Jews. He was not a nice guy.

Read Matthew 2:1-18.

The Magi ended up in Jerusalem chatting with King Herod, asking him where the Christ Messiah was born. Herod became disturbed by this news and deceived the wise men into thinking he wanted to also worship Jesus. His real goal? To kill him. Fortunately, God knows and sees everything. God protected Jesus and kept him safe from the evil king.

What amazes me is that God still loves King Herod. Despite his evil nature and how much sin and sadness he causes in the world, God still loves him. The baby Jesus he tried so hard to find and kill, eventually died on the cross to save King Herod from his sin.

John 15:12 tells us to love people around us just like God loves us. Wow. What a challenge. We are to love everyone around us, not just the easy people to love. Just like God loved King Herod, even though he was not nice, we are called to do the same: always love others.

V is for Villain: the Bad Guy of the Bible

1. Do you have a King Herod in your life? Is there someone who is challenging for you to love? Spend time praying for that person, for God to transform his or her life by His love.
2. If you can't think of anyone in your life who is an enemy, pray for people in the world who are hurting Christians. Pray for people who want to kill those who love Jesus, just like King Herod.
3. Read Luke 6:27-36. Write some of the verses from this section of Scripture to remind yourself how God wants you to treat your enemies.

W is for White: Washed Pure

It rarely snows around Oregon in the valley where I live. When it does snow, it is a big deal. All the schools shut down, and most people cannot make it to work. My family frequently walks around the neighborhood when it snows. We spend some time bundling up and adding layers of scarves, gloves and sweaters before journeying out of the garage. When we finally step outside, all we see is a sea of white, everywhere. The clean, untainted landscape makes me think of purity – something untouched by dirt or grime and free from contamination.

The Bible talks about snow in Psalm 51:7. The Bible talks about how with Jesus, we can be washed white as snow. Our sins are red, but Jesus has cleansed us. Snow represents purity, which is how Jesus entered the world as an innocent little baby. Jesus also left the world pure and untainted by sin because he is the Lord. He is perfect.

As we think about snow in the Bible, it is also interesting to reflect about how snow is made. Did you know snow is created out of crystals that have formed around dirt? How funny that something as beautiful as snow is really made from dirt. That's like us, too. God created us as beautiful creatures, but we are not perfect. We have dirt on us, too, called sin. When we cry out to Jesus and ask for his forgiveness, we are washed clean. We turn into people white and pure as snow.

W is for White: Washed Pure

1. Try to leave as much white space on this page as possible, but journal about what purity means to you. How can you focus on purity this Christmas?
2. Write a prayer asking God to forgive you for your sins.
3. Read Psalm 51. This Psalm was written by David after he realized his sin with Bathsheba. What verses stand out to you from this passage of Scripture?

X is for XOXO: Two-Armed Hugs

December 26th: When I was growing up this day of the year was almost more exciting than Christmas because it meant we got to celebrate with my dad's side of the family. My parents are not divorced, but long ago my dad's siblings decided to get together on the 26th so they could spend Christmas day with others in their families. When I was little, I especially loved spending time with my older cousins, aunts and uncles.

Every year when one particular uncles would walk through the door or leave at the end of the evening, we would give him a hug. Since we didn't normally spend lots of time with him, my sister and I would often give him a "side hug." Then, my uncle would always complain about how we needed to give him a "real" two-armed hug. It made my sister and I giggle as we would hug him again.

Read Acts 20:37.

In this scene of the Bible we see Paul's friends hugging and kissing him because they did not know if and when they would ever see him again. He was getting on a ship and setting off to eventually end up in Rome. His friends showed affection and love to him through hugs and kisses.

I wonder how Elizabeth showed affection toward Mary when Mary returned to her home in Luke 1:56. I wonder how the wise men left Jesus in Matthew 2:12. I wonder how the shepherds left Jesus and his family after visiting them in Luke 2:17. And I wonder how Mary showed affection toward Jesus as he went onto the cross.

X is for XOXO: Two-Armed Hugs

1. Journaling the letters: XOXO What does this phrase mean to you this Christmas?
2. How do you leave events in December? Do you rush out the door? Do you pause and walk around and hug everyone? Think about how your actions are perceived by those around you.
3. Who do you need to embrace and give two-armed hugs to this holiday season? Who can you show love to in that manner? Pray about who God puts on your heart.

Y is for Young: the Unexpected

God often uses the most unexpected people to do big things for His Kingdom. Most people believe that Mary was young when she gave birth to Jesus. Some scholars think Mary was around 14. Think back to when you were 14-years-old. What were you like? Can you imagine being a mother? Can you imagine being a mom to the son of God?

I studied to be a teacher in college, and during my time student teaching, teachers, parents and students all thought I was another high school youth. It made it hard to do my job because people thought I was so young.

As I am writing the *A, B, Cs of Christmas*, I am 26-years-old, but I look like I am still in high school. My mother says I will appreciate having a young face when I get older, but for now I would just like to look my age. I lead the youth program at my church. I never went to seminary, and I had never worked at a church before receiving this job. Many days I feel overwhelmed and underqualified to be able to teach the everyone about Jesus.

I know God has me there for a reason, and just like Mary, I need to remember that God can use anyone to do big things for His kingdom. He does not often pick the people you would think to share the gospel, spread the Good News, and move mountains for Him.

Y is for Young: the Unexpected

1. Who else did God use in the Bible who was an unlikely person for the job? What parts of their lives stand out to you? (Think about David, Rahab, Gideon, Jonah, Paul, Esther, etc.)
2. How are you an unlikely person for God to use?
3. Read and illustrate 1 Samuel 16:7.

Z is for Zzzzz: Rest

The holidays are some of the busiest times of the entire year. From Christmas parties with family to friends to getting gifts for all the neighbors and the people you love... Every day is packed full of activities during the month of December. By the time the end of the season rolls around, I am typically extremely tired.

Read Luke 2:14. Angels are messengers from the Lord, and they are still trying to remind us what it means to have peace and rest in the midst of chaos. You can often find the word "peace" lettered on Christmas cards. Peace means an absence of disturbance or disorder. Peace means tranquility. Those Christmas cards are trying to remind us, just like the angels in the Christmas story, to rest in the Lord.

The Hebrew word for peace is *shalom,* which has a much deeper meaning. Shalom means an inner peace or completeness. A wholeness that can only come from the Lord. When we are resting in the Lord, we can feel a complete sense of calm because He is with us in the middle of the chaos. Shalom does not depend on outer circumstances. It comes from the inside, from our relationship with God.

Z is for Zzzzz: Rest

1. Think about how next December you can make the whole holiday season restful. Brainstorm some ideas about how you can do that and journal them on this page.
2. Now that Christmas is over, how can you head into the new year full of peace and shalom from the Lord? Write a prayer to the Lord asking for His help.
3. Did you receive any Christmas cards from people with the word "peace" on it? Cut them up and glue them onto this page!

Bibliography:

C is for Sugar Cookies: Sweet to Trust in Jesus
Hawn, C. Michael, *History of Hymns: 'Tis So Sweet to Trust in Jesus*. Retrieved from https://www.umcdiscipleship.org/resources/history-of-hymns-tis-so-sweet-to-trust-in-jesus

F is for Frankincense: the Meaning behind the Oil
Axe, Josh (2018, June 30). *What Is Frankincense Good For? 8+ Essential Oil Uses & Benefits for Healing.* Retrieved from https://draxe.com/what-is-frankincense/

I is for I Heard the Bells on Christmas Day: Peace in Troubled Times
Taylor, Justin (2014, December 21). *The True Story of Pain and Hope Behind "I Heard the Bells on Christmas Day."* Retrieved from https://www.thegospelcoalition.org/blogs/justin-taylor/the-story-of-pain-and-hope-behind-i-heard-the-bells-on-christmas-day/

Bibliography:

Q is for Quest: Journeying with Jesus
Guzik, David (2018). *Jesus' Birth and Boyhood.* Retrieved from https://enduringword.com/bible-commentary/luke-2/

The Journeys of Mary and Joseph. (n.d.). Retrieved from http://www.biblestudy.org/maps/the-journeys-of-mary-and-joseph.html

T is for Town: Imagining Ourselves in Bethlehem
Morgan, Robert J, *Then Sings My Soul,* Nashville, TN: Thomas Nelson, 2011, p. 167

V is for Villain: the Bad Guy of the Bible
Zavada, Jack. (2018, September 24). *King Herod the Great: Ruthless Ruler of the Jews.* Retrieved from https://www.thoughtco.com/herod-the-great-enemy-of-jesus-christ-701064

W is for White: Washed Pure
Tobin, Declan. (2018). *Fun Snow Facts For Kids. Easy Science for Kids.* Retrieved from http://easyscienceforkids.com/how-is-snow-made/

Christmas Bucket List

Christmas Bingo Board

Go for a walk and look at Christmas lights	Send a friend some Christmas themed happy mail!	Have a Christmas movie night	Wear only red and green clothing for a day	Create a countdown to Christmas: paper chains or an Advent calendar are good ideas!
Paint your fingernails Christmas colors	Think about a way to bless the staff at your church who are working on Christmas Eve or Christmas day	Hang sparkly lights somewhere in your home	Hunt for a Christmas tree! Outside or in a store. Even if you already have one, wander and look!	Make a Christmas wreath or swag to hang on your front door
Give a police officer a Christmas card	Go ice skating	FREE SPACE	Drink hot apple cider	Make a wreath and hang it on your door, or gift it to a neighbor
Burn a Christmas scented candle	Write out a Christmas Bible verse and put it in a public place for someone to find	Invite someone unexpected over for hot chocolate	Donate your precious time to serve a local charity	Finish the A, B, Cs of Christmas book!
Make or find an ornament to give to a friend	Eat a candy cane	Bake Christmas cookies	Have a Christmas Bible journaling meet up in person or online	Buy crazy Christmas socks for yourself

Made in the USA
Middletown, DE
11 May 2023

30411960R00038